"*The Simplicity of My Soul*"

Recreating My Soul Through Poetry

By Pat Thomas

PublishAmerica
Baltimore

ISBN: 1-60474-567-3
PUBLISHED BY PUBLISHAMERICA, LLLP
www.publishamerica.com
Baltimore

Printed in the United States of America

BOOK DEDICATION:

"I dedicate this collection of poetry to the oldest spirit I know—
my youngest daughter—Katie,
and to my first daughter—Courtney,
who are both my strength and my heart song."

Table of Contents

All of Me

*Written for a special soul that I met, but was never given the opportunity
to express all the love I felt for him.*

Heart, soul and mind, I invite you inside—
To share with you the treasures that are yours to find.

Let me give you a map—we'll begin with my heart,
Where I hold so much love, it's where my feelings for you start.

Feelings of love that turn into happiness so complete,
Touching, sharing, being, caring—is what makes our hearts beat.

From there you touch my soul—you'll find honesty and trust
And hope for tomorrow—strong from dawn to dusk.

Last, you enter my mind, with logic and reasoning
That will give you understanding to complete your being.

There you have it! Heart, soul and mind,

That is all of me—where what you need is yours to find.

Let's Talk About Love

Let's talk about all my soul makes up,
Everything my pen can write down about love.
My pen can't move fast enough—I can't keep up,
Because my soul takes over—and wants to write about love!

My soul goes crazy—it has so much to say,
That it can't all be said—not all of it today.
So I write—just as fast as I can,
Because my goal is to let it all be said.

I give in—in these times—when I am blessed,
My hand is merely an instrument.
I don't question as to the reason why,
The unknown takes over to justify.

I love—love—in it's complete being,
There is nothing anywhere that is more worth seeing
Than love—in the raw—it is life in itself,
And the only thing that defines our self worth.

Thank you for this gift.........

Love
My soul always wonders…

Where does love come from, and how do we know
When to feel it, and when to let it go.
We give it away to those that don't want it,
We hide it, we lose it, we hoard it, we flaunt it.

I will choose to live within it each day
My heart beats by the light of its ray.

It is my existence.

That One Someone

I've heard it said before—we all have our match,
Is this special connection soul to soul?
And why? And when? Where does it come from?
From nowhere?! And how are we supposed to know?

Most of the time then—does fear chase it away?
Who are those that are wise enough to stay?
Is it connected to stages of evolution?
Different planes, different places—what is the solution?

Help me to understand...

I Want Him to Say to Me...

When I meet my soul mate…

You are free to love me, free to put aside your fear,
We have both walked the earth, only—to be right here.
Now that we have found each other—let's explore love,
Let's take it to the highest plane; let's soar above the clouds!

There are no limits—at least, not with me and you,
We've searched for each other endlessly, to find the one heart that's true.
We've been through many others, that we are now completely prepared,
To spend our lives together, all our days, endless love we will share.

We have finally found one another…

The Unexpected
Such a child-like state…

The unexpected is what makes life fun,
when something great happens
The clouds clear—and out comes the sun.
So you bask and enjoy it and wonder how,
something so wonderful can be easy—
Can be experienced in the here and now.

I'm talking about happiness,
the kind a new special someone can bring
That puts a spring in your step and
makes you want to dance and sing.
New love—is there anything that compares?!

The Wizard of Oz Is

Written when my soul was awake...

My favorite movie as a little girl
I still watch again and again to this day.
To think that Dorothy had all along,
The same power that we have when we pray.

Clicking her heels so home she could go
And believing the act would take her there,
Much like the process I'm going through now,
Knowing I can—If only I dare.

It's desire that leads me,
And faith that will take me—
To the place my soul dreams of,
And knows it should be.

For I—like Dorothy—know of a place,
That this process is leading me to,
A place that is love and goodness and grace,
And is filled with nothing but the truth.

My Child—My Prayer

Written from the love in my heart...

Your smile, your touch, your laugh,
Your love—

Look at how much you've grown.
The love in you that you give to me,
A gift that only heaven has known.

I thank the Lord when I touch
Your face,
When I see you run and play,
When you come to me in the middle of the night,
For comfort and a warm and safe place.

Let me stop the world from turning
Long enough to see,
This precious gem that I've been given,
Is so very dependent on me...

Let me be, Lord, all that she needs,
With all my impurities—
Let her grow up and be that woman
That you intended and planned for her to be.

You Are My Friend

Written for an Artist with a beautiful soul…

Sometimes we're fortunate to cross the path,
of a soul we were meant to find,
We know them right away by the feeling that simply
looking in their eyes provides.

They are a friend and somehow we know this,
the connection cannot be denied,
For their presence is one so familiar,
one to which our souls long to describe.

But remembering is what re-creates us,
a process we live every second every day,
Familiar souls come and go to remind us,
who we are and from where we came.

You, my friend, are gentle and giving,
you hold truth as your highest thought,
I know and I understand that—
by this world your soul will not be bought.

I respect you, I honor you and I thank you—
and know we will meet again,
For our journey is not complete,
until we all join and become one in the end.

You Thought About Me Today

I miss this person...

You thought about me—I felt you.
Somehow I always know,
I saw you in my dreams. I felt you come
And I felt you go.
I don't know what it is you wanted,
But the connection was real,
Floating like a ghost, leading me to something
You wanted me to feel.

Yet, so much time has gone by—look at me—
Living day to day,
I think about you coming back, but we both know,
It's not for me to say.
You're somewhere locked in my heart, I know better
Than to question the reason,
Sometimes people enter our lives—
Simply to help us through a hard season.

And then they are gone....

Sweet Seventeen
For every daughter's mother…

Funny and sweet daughter, just seventeen years old
Life's path lies before you, which you are so eager to unfold.
I witness you change, like the passing of a season,
Believing and dreaming, and dreaming and believing.

Hold those dreams tight under your pillow at night,
You'll live them one day when your wings take flight.

So many things you'll be as you continue to re-create,
Your soul is alive, and for recognition will wait.
Love who you are—and if you don't—then change
You are made of many rooms that are to be re-arranged.

Keep perfecting your being until you can smile and say
I love and honor myself for who I am today.

Reality Rock

Do you put yourself out there? I do!
Give way too much—all the love inside of you—
Don't know what to hold back, don't know how,
It's got to be all of you—right here and right now.
Then you're just like me…

Spirits like us are free and never learn
The one word NOT in our vocabulary is "yearn"
That's holding back—having what you can't,
And why would we want to put ourselves through that?
We want to fly…

But in doing that—we attract the users,
The controllers, the worthless, the abusers.
They want our wings, because they don't have their own,
And it's our freedom they've seen—but have never known.
They want to fly…

Love is the high almighty—the trick is to not loose sight,
Of what you are made of—hold on with all your might.
It's what we will all come to in the end,
Don't let go of the jewels in your crown, my friend.
Know that we will meet again…

I Am Tired

The process of re-creating...

I am tired—and feeling beat. Yet, there's so much more
For me to complete.
How am I to start my life at 45? Like an old car,
I put myself in drive.
The kids, the house, the job, the bills—
I cross over one mountain, only to see more hills.

I know where I am going, so I keep it in sight.
But I'm tired and lonely—and lose faith in my plight.

If *only* this or if *only* that—maybe then
I would be where I want to be at!
Cross one goal off and go on to another,
But then things change and something else I discover.
This re-creating my soul is draining me;
I'm tired of figuring out who I want to be.

Sometimes I wonder if I'm no one at all,
By the way that I walk, only to go back to a crawl...

I Am Not Tired

My soul is rejoicing...

The load gets heavy, but I will not quit,
For only to myself must I commit.
Things to be done and experiences to live,
I must find out how much I have to give!

I recognize the things that I am not,
And celebrate discovering what I've got!
To grow tired now would be such a shame,
Why—I've just begun to participate in the game!

This game called life can be so much fun,
The best part is knowing that it's never done!
We go on and on and experience it all,
From tall to short—to large to small.

Giving is living in my highest truth
And in doing so—I constantly live my root—
Living exactly as who I am meant to be,
Brings me into the light—that much closer to Thee.

Reflection on Rejection

Written for a soul that I truly felt love for but it wasn't received...

Our hearts touched—not knowing the reason why—
Spirits intertwined for a brief moment in time.
The unexpected handed us something special and strong,
For us to decide if it was right or if it was wrong.

Freedom of choice to do with it what we may—
Should we take it for granted—does it come along every day?
It was ours to unfold—to embrace or reject,
We would be the only ones the decision would affect.

Appreciate, nurture, and hold this gift near—
Or ignore it, shut it out, and let it disappear.
Those were our choices, and the one that you made,
Was to give up, walk away, and watch it fade.

You gave what you could—but you had no fight,
Too caught up in your own turmoil to care if we were right.
You were given the blessing of love and received it like a fool,
Too closed off to know you had experienced the exception—
not the rule.

All I can do is feel sorry for you!

Love at First Sight

Still questioning the outcome…

Do I believe in love at first sight? I don't know
If I do…
All I know is I believed in us, after spending a short
Time with you.
You came gently into my life, much like mist from
The ocean air
A loving memory of a walk on a beach, during a time
That I didn't have a care.

But the walk became a jog as the clouds turned dark overhead
Elation became anxiety, the mist—hard rain,
And the joy to dread.
Why did you run away, my love? Weren't we as one—didn't we
Feel so right?
Why then am I alone and left to walk
On this desolate beach night after night.

I think of you always and wonder how you're doing
Wonder what your life is like,
Knowing what we could have become together—
had we kept walking
Hand in hand on the beach that night.

I still miss you even now…

Mystic

What every soul loves…

Mystic seeps through the mountains of Sedona,
To refresh the weary and strengthen the weak,
Spend the day there with someone who is special
And indulge yourself in a long over due treat.

Walk up the red rocks, feel the wind on your face,
The sun on your back and the light on your soul
Awaken your sense of wonder and joy—
Breathe it in and the mystic behold.

Incredible Skies

Have you been out west—seen the sunset?
Then you know what I mean—looks like a dream.
A painting so perfect—just sit mesmerized,
By the gift of such an incredible sky.

Take time to appreciate...

Contemplation

My soul wants to go home…

Death cannot be the opposite of birth
They are both evolutions that take place on this earth.
Life then must be everything that happens in between,
The *now* of our soul existing as a human being.

Do we strive for the love and the light from which we came?
And what happens when we get there and win the game?
Do we play another on a higher more complex level?
What happens to those that believe there's an end, a hell, a devil?

If I believe there's no beginning, no end, just now,
That only God knows where I'll go and when and how,
Then is my purpose here to recreate my soul
With love, goodness and truth playing the lead role?

Freedom of choice has got to be the key,
Because all opposite experiences we will eventually be,
And from those moments choose the good—choose love,
Every second, every minute, every day—rise above.

The Happy Girl Inside Me

I was happy as a child, before I experienced reality.
Had no idea where life's journey was going to take me.
But here I am, years later, still innocent—asking why,
I can't come to some kind of peace with myself and with my life.

Why is everyone I meet attaching themselves to my wings?
Why can't they let go—be real—and go with their feelings?
When will I meet someone like me—from the same place?
I want that spirit to love me, and my past to erase.

Someone is just like me—and will give to no end,
When can I meet him—where is he—my life long friend.
Is he looking for me too? I have to believe such,
Because even without knowing him, I love him so much!

So many imposters, so much hurt I have felt,
Where is that heart at—the one I will connect with and melt?
He won't make promises—there will be no need to,
We will know when we see each other—our love will be true.

I want to know him…

My Enemy

Wrtten by my soul at a time when I didn't know me at all…

My enemy is easy to see,
My enemy is me.
And my enemy won't let me be,
She hurts everyone dear to me.

It's not intentionally
For she wears her heart on her sleeve.
Thinking she's protecting me,
She acts erratically.

Not doing anything specifically,
Other than running people away from me.
Such a sharp tongue has she,
Letting feelings of rejection run free.

Turning feelings into words that cut deeply,
Letting those words flow freely.
Not giving the mind a chance to intercede,
Until I'm alone again—just me.

Is Our Love

Like a sleeping flower in the night,
tucked in and completely out of sight,

Is our love…

The dew nurtures it, giving it strength, pedals slowly open—
one by one they grow in length,

Is our love…

Sunlight begins to shine through, little by little—
evaporating the dew,

Is our love…

Suddenly in bloom…For all to see…

Family

You gotta love them—no matter what—
Your family is where your heart comes from,
No matter where you go or what you do,
You can't run away from your start.

They are them, and you are you—
Different, but again, so much the same,
It doesn't matter how far you go,
It's all about—from where you came….

Where did I come from?

We Knew the World's Tallest Man

Written for my Dad's funeral—
My soul remembering the gifts he brought me...

All his children waited by the window each evening
For the tallest man to grace the door,
To climb his body to the top and touch the ceiling
Only to be gently guided back to the floor.

This tall man stood for dignity and grace
And his children never doubted the love in his face.
His legs were bruised as he took off his boots,
Yet another long day, instilling our roots.

As we five grew from the loin of this man,
He never failed to want to understand.
But only if the truth was on our side did we dare
Ask him to go the distance and to be there.

Righteousness, love and goodness led this man
Through the trials and tribulations that completed God's plan.
His inner strength that seemed to touch every hand
Will forever be our salute to the World's Tallest Man.

A Reason Why

Written from the depths of my soul when my Dad passed away.

Within the confinement of these four walls
I search for answers out of my reach.
To put the lesson into perspective,
That the shadow of death is trying to teach.

My soul is empty, my heart is sad,
The ground is shaken beneath my feet.
My breath, my blood, my very being,
Came from the man whose heart doesn't beat.

There were too many things left unsaid,
Why did he go, did he want to leave?
I thought I'd have a second chance,
To be the daughter he wanted me to be.

Of the things that he taught me,
Does he know what I threw out; does he understand what I kept?
Does he know how much he gave to me,
By the tears on my face when he left?

There's got to be a living lesson in all of this
But it seems such a big part of me has died.
I cannot accept this tragic end,
Unless someone can give me a reason why…

The Sorrow of My Soul

Written when my Dad died—
My soul continued to express it's sadness...

The lessons I've learned, like a river run deep,
Their twists and turns crawl around me in my sleep.
Throwing my wrong turns at me until I weep
Taunting me to follow down a dead-end street.

Where did you go, Dad, and why so angrily?
Why can't you seem to make peace with me?
Am I still not who you expected me to be?
My spirit continues to mourn, and mourn desperately.

I look to the sky and feel so alone,
Longing to know everything about your new home,
But the answers for me remain unknown.
Your soul seems distant and cold as a stone.

I'll never let go of my love for you
I want your spirit to be a part of all I do.
See who I am, forgive me, and love me too.
Believe this Father's daughter's heart is true.

Eyes That Didn't See

God replies to my Soul...

So many young and innocent memories
Of my soul not being able to agree,
With their teachings and their beliefs
How was it I was in the midst of this family?

You knew you came from something higher
You loved to sing church songs about me,
Your earliest desire was to go home
Because you knew that was where you would be happy.

It didn't take long for life to cloud that
Darkness, untruth and misery—
Surely home was a place I imagined,
And a place that would probably never be.

You stepped away from and out of the light,
How far down you can't recall,
What you measure as years went by—
Your soul wrote of the downfall.

Through poetry it was written down
I have a collection of it all—
You whispered to me of a talent,
And I chose not to heed the call.

Anger Management

God answers more of my soul's outcry...

Now the truth is spread wide open
Did I ask for this unconsciously?
Why offer up the answers now,
When I have begged before for you to talk to me!

You curse the unseemliness of it all
Where was I when you were 24?
Let me answer you directly—
Did you not hear me knocking on the door?

Why did I wait for your command?
I got none, so in rebellion I turned away.
Determined I already had the answers,
It would make no difference what you had to say.

In an instance I made you 24 again—
In every sense you became that memory,
You lived it again in its fullness
And you couldn't believe what you didn't see!

I began to weep from the shame,
Feeling so bad for what I had done!
Like magic the anger dissolved from my being,
Just like dew on grass dissolving in the sun.

God Has Come

And continues to talk to my soul…

God comes to me—even though I'm strong,
I'm not strong enough—because he never backs down.
All I know is how powerful he is.
Nothing before has made me react like this.

He answers my questions directly, I look at him standing firm—
And know that I need to listen, to things that I so have to learn.

I am amazed each time he comes to me!
Doubt and mistrust are all gone—
Replaced by belief and excitement, this light—
for a lifetime I have longed!

He didn't make me—but I am ashamed.
I weep for the place I am from—
How sad and uncreative, and such a long long way from home.

To another—I might appear crazy, but I tell you—he has come,
And more magnificent than we imagined.
He is the Great I Am—the Holy One.

My prayer is that he appears to all, so they may feel such glory—
The whole world could be happy, what a beautiful end to the story!

What a beautiful life we've been given!

Oh, How I Love Jesus

Written by my soul expressing it's only need before I knew it—
To get back home…

I sit contemplating my life, humbly, in the dark of this night,
From beginning to the present,
and am encompassed by my Savior's light.
Knowing that at a very young age, on this earth I didn't belong,
And as the darkness tries to own me, he, again,
protects me against its wrong.

He whispers—endure just a little bit longer,
the hate, the hurt, the pain,
For the Father is preparing your home,
he has promised to reconstruct your wings.
But as I sit in the still of this night,
my blessings I can so plainly see,
I understand that my Lord in heaven,
wants life here to be easier for me.

My Lord how you continue to love me,
sending angels to protect and surround,
And although I've made some bad choices,
my eyes have stayed heaven bound.
You know I've walked my journey, surely my end is near,
I've played the role you asked of me,
right or wrong, as I feel a tear.

Because He First Loved Me

I don't mean to seem ungrateful, this journey hasn't been in vain,
Although I doubted you when my daddy died,
and my heart overflowed with the pain.
Pain I'll never get over, he wasn't great—but he was good,
Didn't guide me as you intended, but he did the best he could.

Don't hold it against him, Father—
I never did, because I understood,
You placed me right smack in that family,
so that I would be all that you knew I could.
This earth has broken my wings.
My spirit cries for my home above,
The Lord soothes my broken spirit,
and refuels my heart with his love.

Than you for the spirits I have met here,
their presence overwhelms my heart,
But you know Lord that I'm impatient,
for us all to gather in your court.
My only need is to get back home; can I laugh,
can I smile, can I sing?
In front of the Almighty's throne,
fulfilling my heart's desire to worship the King.

Madly

For those of us who believe in soul mates...

Life had handed you a situation, no time
For procrastination,
Put your own feelings last, put the
Sorrow in the past
And move on for the sake of your babies.

That's when I met you, and felt your pain.
Soft sky blue eyes full of clouds of rain.
Your partner in life had lost her life
To tumors of cancer that won the fight.

We loved each other like there was no tomorrow,
And for a short time you forgot your sorrow.
But other things blocked our new start together,
And I was the one through the storm could not weather.

I don't know if I brought you more joy than pain,
More laughter than tears, more sunshine than rain
But I loved you madly, I hope that you know,
I should have stayed, but at the time I had to go.

I will always love you"madly" Mr. B.

The Wall Around My Heart...

*Written by my mind at a time when I didn't know
how to let my soul be free...*

It's taken years to build this wall, brick by brick—I've been so proud.
The locked door keeps everyone outside—
until I met you and opened it wide.

You made me think and wonder—and doubt what I had built,
Almost like the very thing I needed,
was what I had tried so hard to keep out.

Didn't know anything was missing, until I looked into your eyes
Right then and there I knew, the wall that I was so proud of was a lie.

It wasn't keeping anyone out, it was merely keeping me in.
It was harboring the fear, the pain, the loneliness and all the rain.

I reacted like a scared child—pushed you away so that I could be safe.
Back to work on my bricks, back down into my comfortable cave.

And that's where I probably should stay...

Inside the Walls of My Heart
Written for a man that made me laugh for a short time…

The walls are torn down, I don't know what to say—
But you're inside now, and I hope you're here to stay.

You came into my life, it was like I started living again—
You breathed air into my being,
and in your eyes I saw a life-long friend.

So much more than my richest dream,
you are what I've always hoped for.
My heart is flooded by your smile,
which touches places no one has touched before.

I've always said a prayer, if the Lord would just decide to bless me,
With a true and complete love,
I would cherish and protect it fiercely.

They say be careful what you ask for,
sometimes the heavens open up,
Almost laughing at your heart's desires,
and filling you up with way more than enough!!

Puppy

How many animals can one house hold? There's too many now—if the
story be told!
My girls talked me into it—I couldn't say no,
to that little bundle of joy—sold!

I looked into your little puppy eyes,
and then you nestled in my neck and cried.
I felt weak—I couldn't even try, to ground my reservations—why?

Filling up on your love's high, I can only sit back and sigh…
I love you, Cody pup…

I Am Not My Judge

There is nothing to judge—as long as I do my best
I can love and be happy with myself,
and forget about all the rest…

If my choice is the best one that I can make, from within my heart
I'll know….I made it in love's sake.

I had to give you up puppy—and I know you're scared…
Somebody please love Cody…
I do…
I always will…

I Miss the Cody Pup

I know you're settling into your new home,
my heart is heavy with thoughts of you,
But for your sake—I'll give you time—
to feel out what is what, and who is who.
If I come to see you now, you won't understand.
You'll be so excited that I've come,
It will only confuse you, and you'll think you're
going back to my home.
But you're not, Cody Pup, you can't.
You have to stay where you are.
My heart aches with missing you, and I hurt to have you so far.
I love you Cody Pup, and I cry—every night—
I long to have you near,
You are my companion—my love—and again,
for you—I shed a tear.

You are an amazing animal...

I'm Coming, Cody Pup

I'm coming to see you, I'm on my way—
I've waited nearly a month—just for this day!
You've settled in your new home, you know you belong. I've given you
time—to adjust to leaving my home.
You couldn't stay here, pup—it just couldn't be. But a miracle came
along—in the best way possibly!
For your new home holds love and plenty of light.
Play all day, pup—be happy—love life!
You have a companion, you have a yard,
and people that love you, near and far.
Now when I come, you will see me and know,
I've come to visit—and not to take you home.
I love you, Cody pup—more than I can understand. For love knows no
limits between animal and man.
It's a universal thing—so much bigger than us all, and I'm so thankful that
my ears are able to hear it's call.

I'm coming, Cody Pup!

Who Are You

What is going on in your life that I can't see,
I'm talking about the part that you're not telling me.
I don't know you—but long to
I want to find out what makes up *you.*

I'm made of love, and it's what I have to share.
I take chances—I put myself out there.
If I find out in the end you're not for real,
I won't regret a second of how wonderful you've made me feel!

What can I do for you? How can I make you smile?
I want to give you so much—come walk with me for awhile…
Go deep into my being and tell me if you like
What you're seeing.

I want to keep all pain from you…

How Do You Go On?

How do you *not*? When things go awry?
Do you quit living until you figure out why?
No you don't—the world continues to spin—
Come on baby—tell me where you've been…

Is there such a thing as a broken heart?
Or is it really just a beginning—a new start?
Let's get excited—let's see what else life holds,
Mysteries, adventures—so much more to unfold.

It's a little scary—you've got to get out there,
Sometimes you feel leery of your soul to bare….
What if you're not accepted—there you are,
And before you know it—you've gone too far.

Don't worry baby—you can reel it back in—
There's nothing you can do that you can't rescind…
People that know you—love you to no end.
And you can always be with a friend…

Sometimes I'm scared…

A Shower of Blessings

I've lived a hard life, that I can't deny,
But God and the Universe have always been on my side!
When I get these showers, all I can do is sigh,
Say *Thank You* every morning, live out and enjoy the high!

It happens to everyone, from time to time,
In their existence—
But some are oblivious, and remain in a state
Of resistance.
Me—I turn my face upward to the sky!
And caress the shower, as I would a drug that makes me high.

We all go down, so that we can appreciate going up!
Ask for help; don't be afraid to extend your cup.
God will fill your needs—answer your every prayer,
And let me assure you, my friend, in the darkness
He will be there…

I love you, Lord…

What Do You Think Now?

I think that I loved—and lost,
I think that my pain shows the high cost.
But yet—look—a glimmer through the clouds,
Didn't you always know—didn't you have no doubt—

You knew it would come back around,
because what you lost—would in time
Be found.
It's called faith—it's a gut feeling
It's something that sends you reeling—

The feeling is too strong to disappear—you knew it wasn't lost
Out of fear.
It's real and it has to make a stand,
You hear the music playing by the band!

Where do you go from here?
Do you dare to dream—do you let loose of your fear?

What about him—will courage lead?
Or are you on another dead end street?

Time will tell……..

I Know, Grandma

I know, Grandma. I watched you. You're tired.
Feeling like your time on this earth has just about expired.
Let me tell you how selfish I am…

I want to see your eyes twinkle again, every time you smile. I want to walk
through the woods with you,
And stop and look at a snapping turtle for awhile.

I want us to drive through the mountains,
take your picture next to an Indian Chief,
I want the car to knock through Knoxville, just one more time—let's look
at a turning leaf.

I want you to tell me how Pa loved me,
keep him alive for me—just once more.
And I want to tell you I love you—again and again,
before you get to heaven's door.

My book of poetry is something you'll never see,
so I'm giving you the gift of my soul,
Right here—I want to share it—right now—
I want you to have it before you go.
I love you Grandma, more than you'll ever know…
And this is the most important poem I'll ever write…

I know, Grandma, I know….

War

My soul mourns for the hurt, the angry, the fearful...

We see the faces on the T.V. screen,
killing in the name of protection,
But how do we know where the line is drawn,
between that and just angry aggression?

What has brought us to this point,
to collectively own so much fear?
That we have to be bigger, meaner than all,
to survive this darkness year after year.

Who have we become so afraid of? In the end—
is it only ourselves?
For if we are truly one in love,
then what has created so much hell?

What would happen if the powerful weapons were turned
to food and medicine and clothes,
Giving all the human race dignity, erasing fear
and anger and woes?

Would love then be our guide? Thoughts
and words then turned to good?
Could we all then live in unity,
the way that truth shows us we should?

One day—one mankind...

The Road from Sister to Friend

And the years that it took to walk...

Two little girls, each as different as they could be,
Mom would dress us alike—trying to blend our identity.
But it didn't work—or did it...
We fought more than we played—laughed more than we cried,
I broke your Barbie's—you broke my arm, we played "I Spy."
I wanted to be big like you....

You witnessed my first kiss, then swore you'd tell on me,
Doing your chores for weeks was my only chance at peace,
You wanted to be kissed like me...

In high school you had the clothes, the friends, the guys,
I was the little troublemaker that didn't exist in your eyes.
I wanted to be popular like you...

You found a career and a husband—I was struggling to find me,
Instead I found the same things too, and thought I was complete.
I wanted to be responsible like you...

You were blessed with children, amid an unhappy existence,
I headed the same direction, but had to end the dance.
You wanted to be brave like me...

So brave you became, left the misery, and set out in a new light,
To reach the same destination as me in this life.
We both want to be happy...

Two grown women, each as alike as they can be
Owe it to a mother that long ago blended their identity.
For I am you, and you are me…

I'm Getting What I've Asked For

Tonight I was able to see a glimpse
Of what my life consists of,
I cry about being lonely, but yet
I ride on the wings of love.

I want to finish my book of poetry,
This I have proclaimed—
Knowing I write best from the feelings,
Of hurt, loss, love and pain!

So alone I must be at this time,
To feel and write and feel,
In order to get where I'm going,
I have to live within what's real.

Thank you, universe! I understand now...

Outspoken Soul

So loud!!

You have so much to say, so I grab my pen,
Anxious for you to tell me where to begin.
Across the paper the emotions begin to spill,
Not worried about correct grammar—just say what you feel.

It's beautiful to me, and such a great release,
To be able to express my heart so openly,
I can only hope that others will find,
Comfort and peace through these words of mine.
My soul loves to write—mostly about love…

Without You

I guess it doesn't matter—that I'm crazy about you—
You were crazy about me—in the beginning,
What happened to you…

The loving touches stopped,
No more—you can't get enough of me,
I feel so strange—like we can't talk,
I want to give you a way out—can't you see.

Don't be with me
If you don't want to…

Irritated

Irritated. By everything. Don't ask me why.
You don't really care, until you see me cry.
The sink's stopped up, the weeds have grown high,
The kid's rooms are a mess, my bank account is dry,
is that enough reasons why?
I'll give you more.

Irritated. By everything. Don't talk to me.
Cut, cut,—keep cutting, til I bleed.
Car needs oil, washer is overloaded, and the D-backs are losing 6 to 3.
Cat is hungry, dog wants out, I don't want to go to the store.
Should I go on—do you still need more?

Irritated. By everything. But, never you mind.
As long as I keep on giving—you can remain blind.
Your friends use me too—and you think that's fine.
Take over my house, take advantage of a nature that's kind.

Get out of my house, I want to be alone,
Nothing would be lost, broken, used or stolen.
I would be the only responsibility I would own,
And for that—I wait to grow old.

How pitiful I am sometimes…

Wake Up

God took the pen out of my hand because he has something to say...

So much spiritual power each of you hold
You must unleash it—every story to be told!
Places to go—so much to see and be,
Wake up—begin now—down the path to your journey!

Listen to the sound of the voice from within,
It's there you'll find guidance and there you are to begin.
Help one another—make that your every step,
Make it your reason for actions—it will give them depth.

Once you understand the concept I've recommended,
You'll see the difference in outcome from what you had intended.
You will begin to glorify yourself, you will glorify me,
Thus starting your journey to all that you can be!

WAKE UP!

Realization

Those dark clouds come—tell me you know what
I'm talking about—
Out of nowhere—replacing confidence
With doubt.

Realizing what we take for granted—then
Boldly showing us its absence—
Turning it into something we could lose,
To quickly give it back its substance.

Nothing is a sure thing—doesn't count how
Comfortable we begin to feel—
We then let taking for granted set in,
Until humbly we look at what is real.

Yes—reality comes knocking in an effort
To keep our feet on the ground,
And to give us the chance to hold tight,
To what we have found.

Yes—hold tight to the things that are dear,
Those things are precious—
Only fools let them go out of fear…

Loving Myself

Sometimes your life becomes surrounded by people, and circumstances
that are unfair,
Every place you turn for support you find,
That it just isn't there.

You've been demoted at your job—
your kids are bleeding you dry.
Friends seem to be distant and few,
so alone into your pillow at night you cry.

Even the love of your life has changed,
and now seems to require "space."
No matter how positive you try to stay—
you just can't seem to keep the faith.

What is happening—you ask yourself—
what have I done to make the tables turn?
So you then look deep inside yourself to figure out
the lesson that needs to be learned.

I have found that I can embrace this time—
for I am re-creating my soul again!
I'm not judging—but rather—loving myself,
for it's there that I always find my best friend!

I will always carry myself on...

I Love When I Can Write

Look at the words that are coming out of me—
When I can write—I am as blessed as I can be!
I know when it hits me—the floodgate is released,
And so my pen moves on until I am so pleased.

By the same token—I know when the gate is closed,
For whatever reason—I can't get anything out of my soul.
Those are sad times, for I long to fill my cup,
But each time I try—I choke and I'm all dried up.

So I know now that my writing is a gift,
Nothing to take for granted—I take it sip by sip.
It is who I am—what I long for—what I do,
It is the one and only thing that makes my life true.

I want to share the soul's treasures with others...

Beautiful Me

You try to bring me into your misery,
But my spirit refuses—beautiful me
None of you can hold me down for long,
I give thanks to be guided by such a gentle song.

We all choose with what to fill our cup,
Knowing when it's wrong, and knowing when we've had enough.
But what exactly is it that we need?
Well—different things—oh yes—beautiful me.

Do you choose the sun, the clouds, the rain?
What about choosing to live within the pain?
Or are you able to release and set your spirit free?
I am—and I do—beautiful me!

I set my spirit free of all misery,
And therefore I am and will be—beautiful me!
I live within the goodness that life holds,
And continue to watch the miracles unfold.

Beautiful me—and so I choose to remain free…

I Choose to Be Happy

That's a personal choice that I make,
I have to reconfirm it every day.
Each and every step I take along the way,
I let the sunlight in—ray by ray.

Some days it's an uphill battle,
And I slip and slide in the saddle.
But as long as I keep the wind on my back,
I know there is nothing in which I will lack.

Happiness is not an illusion—not a dream,
It doesn't have to be as unattainable as it may seem.
Look at it—embrace it—live it,
And you'll find it's exactly what you'll get.

If only there were more positive thoughts
sent out into the universe…

You Own It—I Don't

It's yours—all the pain and suffering,
All the regrets, all the should have beens.
You have to deal with it all,
The times, the seasons, the changing winds.

I trust that you'll get through it,
In the best way that you know how,
And I don't take it personally,
That you can't handle me being around.

Oh sure—easy for me to imagine,
I'd handle it differently than you,
But it's not my reality to control,
It's yours—and I'm certain that you'll get through.

I'm not here to judge you,
And my sadness is for your pain.
It's not for me—not about me—
You're the one that's standing out in the rain.

I only wish you happiness...with or without me...

Standing Out in the Rain

I sit alone with my hand on my chin
Staring out into the dark and cold,
Out my window the rain is coming down,
I can make out a figure, as you slowly unfold.

You're standing there with your hands at your side,
The rain is steadily coming down.
You're defeated, you're drained, and you're all alone,
Lost with no desire to be found.

My heart goes out to you—I feel your pain,
Instantly I want for you to come in—
Get dried, get warmed and sit with me,
Until you feel your strength coming back from within.

But my want—you don't share,
And there's nothing I can do to change your mind.
It's your loss—it's your pain—it's all you,
And the answers—alone—you must find.

I send you love and light…

Emotionally Drained

I know you are—and I feel your hurt, I saw your pain today—
You shut me out, but can't you let just a ray of my
sunshine come your way?

Can't you trust me even enough, to open that door—just a crack—
You don't have to give me anything, I understand you're blue.
Let me give you the love that you've given me in the past,
Right back to you.

You live by a code of ethics, it's black and white—right or wrong.
There's no gray in between, not with you
You follow the rules. But babe, you don't have to be punished
For everything you do.

I don't hold the key to your contentment, but you do,
And I do know that you are worthy of all the
good things inside of you.

Soon there will be another season
In which you will be open to love,
I have faith that you'll get through
I know in time, on your wings you will rise above.

And you'll be such a better person for it!! I love you!!...

Today

I'll always cherish the night we met,
Couldn't see anyone else in the room—they disappeared,
Until only you and I were left.
I thought I should bottle and sell that feeling,
convinced it was so real,
Until we met again, and deeper you touched my being.

And so the pattern began—each day being even more
With me thinking that day was unstoppable,
until the next made a mockery of the day before.
Over time it was in the 'now' I began living,
so thankful for that days blessings,
And yet—loving the anticipation of what tomorrow might bring.

I can only caress this happiness one day at a time,
being thankful that my heart is filled
Just won't let me get beyond loving today—
for today you are mine.
I'm unable to look at one year, five years, ten years,
I can't let go of today,
Because in doing that, I'm sure,
it would only leave me in tears.

And I so want to enjoy and live today
Feel the blessing—be thankful,
Live in this feeling here and now—in every way.

Please don't take today away...I appreciate the way love grows...

Love Always Comes Through
Believe in it...

Sometimes it's hard to understand the outcome,
When love seems to have left you empty and numb.
But if it was meant to be, it'll come back around,
And only then will you know it wasn't lost—but found.

Love doesn't die, no matter how many tears you cry,
Instead, in its own way, it grows with each passing day.
It will leave you shaking your head—so sure it was dead,
But there it is even stronger—holding on even longer.

If you think it was love and wait for its return,
And it fades and fades until the fire no longer burns,
Then you can be sure you had nothing to lose,
Because it wasn't true love—just time that was used.

So be patient my friend, hold steady to the end,
The truth will be revealed—your heart knows what it feels.

Listen to your heart—
Love always comes through

Letting Go

An outsider could look at my life and say
Oh my...

So many things to deal with each and every day
I try...

I could obsess over my situation
I won't...

That would only make me panic and run
I don't...

There's an unseen net that keeps me safe
Thank you...

And I know in this life I have a place
It's true...

I am watched over—like a baby in a cradle
I am safe...

So bring it on world—my boat is stable

No waves!!

Dad

It's been four years now since your death,
And in that time—I feel my life has been blessed.
You'd be proud of me, Dad—I've done things right,
I've taken care of my children—just like you'd like.

This year your death falls on a holiday,
All of us will be together on that day.
You'd like that—the whole family thinking of you,
Giving thanks is what we will all gather to do.

I still have questions unanswered, Dad,
And sometimes I'm alone and I feel very sad.
I miss you and love you very very much,
And wish once more I could feel your touch.

I can't thank you enough for loving me,
And giving me such a strong family history.
Teaching me right from wrong—always being on my side,
Being a part of you always has filled me with such pride.

I'll love you into eternity, Dad...

The Wrong One

I can't hold your poison any longer in my hand,
You've pushed me to my limit—it's all I can stand.
Your reality has no place for me
And all of your negative—I can no longer be.

Let me out of it—deal with your life,
And please don't continue to give me your strife—
I believe now that you are not who I thought you were,
Instead I can now see the misery at your door.

And that's how you live—that is the truth of you,
You are meant to be sad, you are meant to be blue.
But me—I love sunshine—I look for the good,
To live a happy life—is something everyone should.

So let's just be glad that our paths crossed,
And I don't regret any time that's been lost.
For experiencing everyone to me is worth the cost,
And on the ocean of life—we all get tossed.

I wish you the best...

Twists and Turns

So complicated...

Don't we all go through heaven and hell—
We experience it all—just not all of us tell.
Because we don't understand—so we keep it to ourselves,
Our personal torment—not sure what we just felt...

Emotions—man! They can run the gamut! Leave us confused,
Who caused this confusion—dammit!
Relations with others—puts us through it
You think you're smart enough not to do it!

What About Me and My Rain

You're out in the rain and you've left me alone,
I'm trying to keep myself happy—trying to go on.
But babe—the truth is—I miss you desperately,
And these nights alone are killing me.

I'm up one day—I'm down the next,
I understand/I don't understand how you feel,
I put your feelings first and know that you hurt,
But then comes my rain and all the pain that I feel.

Where can I go to be happy?...

When There's No One

When there's no one—are you afraid—are you alone?
Are you uncertain—uncomfortable even at home?
Or can you get out amongst them—table for one,
Can you walk with confidence—even with no one?

Let me tell you something that has to do with strength,
You are the only one with which you'll go the length.
Love yourself, accept yourself—see who you are,
And then know and feel inside that you are a star!

Weed out the unwilling, the non accepting, the wrong,
And only let in those that have a beautiful song.
Be it a person—be it an animal—but be it true,
If you listen, your heart will never deceive you.

You don't faze me…
And I am not cold. I am so real…

Cupid's Arrow

I've been hit before in various places,
By that infamous arrow, leaving marks and traces
All over my body…

But this was aimed right at my heart and didn't miss,
Filling me with such an enormous dose of bliss
I don't know how I'll use it all…

I'm scared of losing ground
So many responsibilities—I have to be sound
Or do I…

A man I can't live without—hasn't that been my dream?
Then I have what I want—doesn't it seem?
What frightens me about loving him?
It is a game that I don't think I can win?

He's wonderful…

My Brother

"It's not my house, It's not my wife's house,
It's my house, her house, and your house."
She's not heavy, she's my sister...

A friend through my childhood, and even closer
Now that we're grown
I love the beauty of him, surrounded—but mostly
When we're alone.
Because when we're alone I see everything that he can be,
All of his beauty shines and there is none of him that I can't see.
I feel so proud to know him, but more so—
To know of his love,
And be a part of the light, that only some can see glow.
He is my brother and my soul knows his goodness is true.
Wherever his path leads him, no doubt the truth
Will always come through.

I love you John...

Who I Am

I could tell stories of a lonely little girl
that would surely make you cry,
But she's not who I am,
only what I've experienced in this life.
So I won't...

My Future

Pen in hand—I thank you once again—
You lead—I follow—all of my tomorrows…

I will trust in the light, for you know what's right…
For my heart and soul…

Thank you…